Nature's Pep Talk

AF632796

Abinaya Ayyamperumal

BookLeaf Publishing

Presentation by *BookLeaf Publishing*

Web: www.bookleafpub.com

E-mail: info@bookleafpub.com

ISBN: 9789357211468

First edition 2022

DEDICATION

To

My Dad

who encouraged me to always believe in myself

My Mom

who had always seen my scribbled snippets as best selling books

My Sister

who placed heavy onus on me through her multi-talented footprints

My Husband

who is my sounding board whose constant support and motivation in whatever I do

I could not repay

But I'll try anyway,

My children

for being my loudest cheerleaders without whom this collection would be published 2 years later.

My friends

for their unending love and support.

ACKNOWLEDGEMENT

I thank the bookleafpublishing team for their inspiring initiative to help writers like me to accomplish our long unredeemed dreams turn into reality.

I thank all my teachers for instilling in me the roots of writing passion.

I thank all writers whose books shaped my childhood memories into unswerving inspiration to become a writer.

PREFACE

Life is very beautiful and the world is glowing everyday with immense beauty for all humans and living beings without any discrimination.

Nature is disappearing in front of our very eyes everysecond that we miss to enjoy and also forget that the nature's gifts we relished in our childhood is no more available to our children and grandchildren.

Our life has been witnessing the vanishing of wild mammals,butterflies,mayflies, songbirds and much more.
But,we buckle under the problems of day-to-day life with whimpers.

How can we enjoy this beautiful life without devoting our time to fears,frets and regrets?

The nature in itself comes to us with a pep talk,teaching us life lessons through it's own life experience on earth in different forms

Trees

Allow me to teach you non-resistance
As seasons change,people change what they said.
Learn gladly the art of acceptance
For seldom is the autumn beauty,if my leaves
resist turning red!

When winter arrives on silent feet
I never hold my leaves captive,
Letting go isn't about loss nor defeat
It is to cherish the beauty of subtractive!

Remember your roots,never bypass
For strength and valor it always brings,
Give your children these two gifts
One is roots and the other is wings!

Ocean

Everything that belongs to you, will eventually come
If you create the capacity to receive it,
For boundless are the depth and mysteries
Of a human heart and my pit.

If I can calm by myself,so can you
Be cool and let your light shine,
For we are both salt and water
Mixed with air and soaked in brine.

Every drop of water and grain of sand
Is what I am,you see as Mighty Ocean,
Every deed of kindness,little moments in land
Makes the complete human potion!

Sunrise & Sunset

We have strong power to heal your soul
If you try to visit us in between
All it takes is just one good stroll
To get your mind & body a deep clean!

Storms,turbulents and thunders may come
Yet we never cancel our golden shows
To problems & pressures never succumb
Enjoy every moment that life bestows!

As dark as your heart gets
It is best if you just say no
For there is no sunrise if not the Sun sets
Promises it brings,you never know.

Sky

When life gets hard and you feel let down
Look up at me,you are not alone,
For many woeful beings than you right now
Breathing under the firmament I enthrone.

I may look bleak and empty
But I withhold many gifts within,
The Sun,the Moon,meteors and every entity
Reminds us-every new day life shall begin!

No matter what storms are passing
Know that it's a transient scene,
Beyond the clouds of crisis,
The Sun is shining in the blue between!

Sun

I make unwavering appearance
Everyday for you to grow
Harness my light all day
For soon you see I go

Unfeigned commitment is all it takes
To always be of use to the world
Revel in the life of gracious giving
Rather,a receiving heart unfurled.

Look around you in all relations
For something to always give
Not to hurl them accusations
Nor await for what you can receive.

Stars

Never succumb to the world's darkness
Be radiant and shine your inner light,
Letting yourself to twinkle fearless
For a star is brightest in the darkest night.

Endless opportunities around you to embrace
Akin to the stars in the firmament
Just find your stage in the outer space
For options to choose are never permanent.

With intentional beams of starlight
Come on,inspire others to be superstars
For more brighter is the darkest night
When working together as tiny stars!

Mountain

Majestic and poised is my stance
Open and wild for you to hike
Under the humongous ball of fire
Never will I slump for a thunderstrike
Tread carefully on the road you take
Admire the beauty around you
It's ok to slow down and take a break
Nourishing your soul with my
Snow-capped strength under the blue!

Wind

Not all things present can be seen or heard
Some things need to be felt
Never trust only the beauty-a byword
Lest,you let your heart melt!

You can't judge me by my cover
Still you take me as I am
Why don't you exert human power
To accept people as gentle as a lamb!

Learn from me the act of moving
It's easy to sit and relax
Success is crowned with process and grooming
When comfort zone is given the axe!

Animals

Tigers and zebras share the stripes
Yet they differ as black and white
Zebras don't envy at tiger's gripes
And wish to hunt like the tiger might.

Accept yourself as you are
Know your own fortes and flaws
Embrace your beauty and not compare
Each one is unique for a cause!

Learn amazing habits from us
We are all around you
We never change our nature
As humans so often do.

We also live in mud
Some live to freeze in snow
We adjust even in plains
Where humans just come and go.

Life is gifted to just adapt
And repent in vain
For each got just one to act
To smile in spite of pain.

Bird

Freedom is awaiting me
In that brilliant beaming sky
Soaring high when set free
I seldom fear to fly high!

Ward off your fear when besieged,
Spread your wings,it's time to fly…
Failure is not whether you have peaked
It is when you miss the chance to try.

Rain

Rain may call off our plans
At some point,withers our hopes
In Spite of being a spoilsport,it
Nebulizes the famished farmers
Yearning to quench their crops…
Do our setbacks appear abound
Amidst the praying hands?
Yet we fret for something bigger
Searching for grassy lands.

Clouds

Clearer is the sky that

Lies behind your cloud of thoughts

On the backdrop of our mind

Unfolding the memoirs & the foresights,

Dwell only on the present,for that

Shall soon too pass!

Rainbow

Colors borrowed from God's own palette
To paint the human's sphere
With celestial greens in colorful salad
Rainbow regime is healthier!

Everything is not as appears to be
Do not presume upon your sight
Even I am not an arch you see
But a full circle braw and bright!

Autumn

A touch of cold in the swaying tree
And touch of gold in the ruddy moon
The wind is dancing in fun and glee
To the gusty garden's tune.

Time to harvest and success
Of all the days of labor
It's time to rest and rejoice recess
Do yourself a favor!

Colorful leaves getting ready to paint
All the worrisome looks that preps to faint
Drench in the colors for white is coming
New year spirits, keep it running!

September lessons

I went to the woods on a bright
golden hour of autumn
Away from the summers angry eye
with nothing to tether me to this world…

To realize the power of my vision…
To realize the power of hearing…

And feel the breeze caress through the leaves
to the soft music of the creeks……...

I realized that life is not to be wasted on the past
nor fear of future,
But to just walk in the woods all through
september!

November lessons

The clouds are grey and promise
Winter for a good storm
We love to cuddle inside
By the fire to keep warm.

Squirrels are busy storing
Priceless oaks for weeks,
Lazy bones busy snoring
on the pillow with buried cheeks.

The period of thanksgiving
to dear ones and God
Nature is terribly so forgiving
For the paths we have trod.

Butterflies

Believe that life is too short
Understand that we constantly change from
The moment we are born,
The evolution of a butterfly
Embodies lifecycle of ours in every stage
Resisting the change never helps
For leading the happiest
Life is always
In our hands to
Enjoy every
Stance!

Garden

Plant your seeds of hope today
Nourish them with love and care
Weariness you just put away
To relish your harvest share.

A seed sprouts at it's right time
It grows not by edgy force,
Giving up halfway is a crime
Be patient to ingest the incense rose.

Bamboo Tree

I don't show any signs of growth
Over the years strengthening my roots
Although it seems too easy to loathe
Developing your inner strength troubleshoots.

Other trees grow tall in a few months
Before I even begin to sprout
Have faith in yourself is my two cents
Focus on others can cause you burn-out!

Be patient and nurture your dreams like me
Work on the foundations from within
I shoot up 90ft in weeks you see,
Consistency led my life to begin!

Plant Trees

Go and plant a tree
When you are still young
So you will have them statuesque
When you walk among!

When you plant a seed
You set the stage for a life,
For species in earnest need
Bolstering varied wildlife.

When you are aging
You can walk in shade
And exult in gloating
That you and nature made!

Nature

Nourish your soul with my

Adorable gifts and wishes

That I provide to you every micro seconds

Under the sky, not everything is

Recurring for you to miss but

Everlasting is my generous love to mankind.

www.ingramcontent.com/pod-product-compliance
Lightning Source LLC
Chambersburg PA
CBHW051718130826
49812CB00034B/1234
* 9 7 8 9 3 5 7 2 1 1 4 6 8 *